ZUCCHINI COOKERY

ENLARGED EDITION OF ZUCCHINI COOKBOOK

BY

VIRG AND JO LEMLEY

WILDERNESS HOUSE
11129 Caves Highway
Cave Junction, OR 97523

© copyright 1976 by WILDERNESS HOUSE
ISBN 0-931798-02-7

WILDERNESS HOUSE BOOKS

- **CHILDREN'S COOKERY — NATURALLY**
  NOW CHILDREN HAVE FUN LEARNING
  TO COOK WITH FOODS THAT ARE
  BEST FOR THEM.

- **SOYBEAN COOKERY**
  BEAT TODAY'S RISING FOOD COSTS.
  LEARN TO COOK DELIGHTFULLY
  APPETIZING, ALL—AMERICAN
  DISHES FOR PENNIES.

- **ZUCCHINI COOKERY**
  BURIED IN ZUCCHINI? THIS IS
  THE BOOK FOR YOU.

AT WILDERNESS HOUSE——

EACH MEAL IS NEVER QUITE THE SAME AS THE LAST BECAUSE OF DIFFERENT INGREDIENTS IN THE HOUSE AND A CULINARY SENSE OF ADVENTURE.

HERE ARE SPECIFIC RECIPES: EACH USED MANY TIMES AT WILDERNESS HOUSE. USE THEM — BUT BRANCH OFF AND EXPLORE TO MAKE YOUR OWN DELIGHTFUL NEW DISCOVERIES WITH ZUCCHINI.

WILDERNESS HOUSE ZUCCHINI TIPS

- IF YOU ARE USING ZUCCHINI FRESH, SUCH AS IN SALADS, SANDWICHES, COLD SOUP, ETC,; YOUR ZUCCHINI WILL BE TASTIER IF YOU SOAK IT FOR 30 MINUTES IN 1 CUP WATER AND 1 TEASPOON SALT.

- IF YOUR ZUCCHINI HAS GOTTEN OUT OF HAND AND YOU CAN'T KEEP UP WITH IT, SET UP THE FOOD GRINDER AND HAVE THE FAMILY GRIND AWAY. ONE DAY WE GROUND 24 CUPS! FILL A DOUBLE PLASTIC BAG, TIE, AND TOSS INTO THE FREEZER. FOR BEST RESULTS, DEFROST IN A COLLANDER. THIS IS SO CONVENIENT WHEN YOU WANT TO MAKE BREADS OR PIES IN A HURRY.

- GRATED ZUCCHINI WORKS WELL IN RECIPES THAT CALL FOR GROUND ZUCCHINI, AND ALSO FREEZES WELL.

- IN CASSEROLES YOU CAN USE YOUR LARGE ZUCCHINI, SLICED, BUT IF THE SKIN DOESN'T LOOK TENDER IT'S BEST TO PEEL BEFORE USING.

- IN ALL RECIPES WE FOUND THAT WHOLE WHEAT FLOUR WORKS GREAT. WE'VE ALSO USED HONEY FOR SWEETENING IN MOST CASES.

- IF THE RECIPE CALLS FOR BOILED, PARBOILED, COOKED, ETC., ZUCCHINI — AND YOU HAVE A STEAMER — BY ALL MEANS STEAM THE VEGETABLE AND SAVE THOSE PRECIOUS VITAMINS.

- AT WILDERNESS HOUSE WE LOVE COOKING WITH ZUCCHINI. IT ADDS A UNIQUELY BEAUTIFUL COLOR AND TEXTURE, ENHANCING ANY DISH IT IS USED IN.

TABLE OF CONTENTS

MAIN DISHES

DESSERTS

BREADS

PICKLES AND RELISHES

HOW TO DRY ZUCCHINI
HOW TO FREEZE ZUCCHINI

APPETIZERS

4 FRESH YOUNG ZUCCHINI

CUT ZUCCHINI IN HALF - LENGTHWISE. SCOOP OUT PULP. SPRINKLE SALT OVER THE INSIDE OF THE ZUCCHINI HALVES AND LET SIT FOR 10 MINUTES. BLOT DRY WITH A TOWEL. MOUND FILLING INTO ZUCCHINI HALVES. CUT IN 1 INCH PIECES.

YIELDS: 40 APPETIZERS

DILL FILLING

8 OZ CREAM CHEESE
4 TSP. MINCED PARSLEY
1 TSP. DILL SEED
1/2 TSP. GARLIC SALT
4 TSP. DRIED MINCED ONION
COMBINE WELL

——— OR ———

PICKLE FILLING

8 OZ CREAM CHEESE
3 TBS. SWEET PICKLE RELISH
1/8 TSP. SALT
COMBINE WELL

WILDERNESS COCKTAIL

2 C. TOMATO JUICE
1 TSP. WORCHESTERSHIRE SAUCE
1 1/2 TSP. SOY SAUCE
1/4 TSP. TABASCO
1 TSP. SALT
MAKES TWO CUPS.

MORNING WAKER—UPPER

2 C. WILDERNESS COCKTAIL
2/3 C. CUBED, YOUNG ZUCCHINI

BLEND IN BLENDER. SERVE CHILLED.

ZESTY DIP

    2 C. GROUND ZUCCHINI — DRAINED
    2 TBS. CHOPPED ONION
    1/4 TSP. BASIL
    1 C. WILDERNESS COCKTAIL

    COMBINE IN SAUCE PAN AND SIMMER
20 MINUTES.

PUT IN BLENDER:

        COOKED ZUCCHINI MIXTURE
        2 - 8 OZ. PACKAGES CREAM CHEESE
        DASH CAYENNE PEPPER

        BLEND ON HIGH SPEED UNTIL
SMOOTH. CHILL AND SERVE.

                        YIELDS: 2 1/2 CUPS

GAZPACHO (COLD SOUP)

    1 C. BELL PEPPER FINELY DICED
    2 C. ZUCCHINI, SLICED THIN AND QUARTERED
    1 C. GRATED CARROTS
    1 C. CELERY, FINELY DICED
    1 C. CUCUMBERS, FINELY DICED
    1/2 C. CHOPPED ONIONS
    2 C. WILDERNESS COCKTAIL
    2 TBS. OLIVE OIL

    COMBINE ALL INGREDIENTS AND
MARINATE OVERNIGHT. SERVE CHILLED
IN SMALL BOWLS BEFORE OR WITH YOUR
MEAL.

                    SERVES: 6-8

3

MOCK SPLIT PEA SOUP

3 C. SLICED ZUCCHINI
2 TBS. INSTANT MINCED ONION
1 TSP PARSLEY FLAKES
1 CUBE CHICKEN BOUILLON
1/2 C. LIGHT CREAM

1/2 C. WATER
2 TBS. MARGARINE
2 TBS. FLOUR
1/2 TSP. SALT
1 C. MILK
1/8 TSP. PEPPER
DASH CAYENNE
(SOUR CREAM AND PAPRIKA OPTIONAL)

COMBINE ZUCCHINI, WATER, ONION, PARSLEY, CHICKEN CUBE AND SALT IN A SAUCE PAN. COOK UNTIL ZUCCHINI IS TENDER AND ONLY A SMALL AMOUNT OF WATER IS LEFT. PUT IN BLENDER AND PUREE.

IN ANOTHER SAUCE PAN: MELT MARGARINE, ADD FLOUR, PEPPER AND SALT. BLEND WELL. ADD MILK AND CREAM. SIMMER, STIRRING UNTIL THICKENED. STIR IN PUREE, MIXING WELL. IF SOUP IS THICKER THAN YOU LIKE, ADD ADDITIONAL MILK

YOU MAY SERVE THIS WITH A SPOON OF SOUR CREAM ON EACH BOWL, TOPPED WITH PAPRIKA.

SERVES: 4

HEARTY SOUP

1 PACKAGE LIPTON ONION SOUP
3 C. WATER
2 C. ZUCCHINI - THINLY SLICED

BRING ALL INGREDIENTS TO BOIL. SIMMER FOR 15 MINUTES. SERVE HOT WITH PARMESAN CHEESE SPRINKLED ON TOP.

SERVES: 4

ITALIAN SOUP

1 POUND STEW MEAT
3 C. ZUCCHINI, THINLY SLICED
1 C. BROKEN SPAGHETTI
        (UNCOOKED)
2 TBS. OIL
6 C. WATER
2 CANS (8 OZ SIZE) TOMATO
        SAUCE
1 CLOVE GARLIC, CRUSHED
1   TSP. OREGANO
1 TBS. SALT
1/4 TSP. COURSE PEPPER
2 TBS. CHOPPED PARSLEY
1 ONION, CHOPPED

CUT STEW MEAT INTO SMALL CUBES BROWN IN OIL. ADD ALL INGREDIENTS EXCEPT ZUCCHINI AND SPAGHETTI. SIMMER FOR TWO HOURS. ADD ZUCCHINI AND SPAGHETTI. SIMMER UNTIL SPAGHETTI IS TENDER.

SERVE IN BOWLS AND SPRINKLE WITH PARMESAN CHEESE, IF DESIRED.

SERVES: 6-8

5

LUMBERJACK SOUP

1 1/2 POUNDS ZUCCHINI
1 ONION — CUBED
1 BELL PEPPER—CUBED
1/2 POUND MUSHROOMS
1 SMALL HEAD CAULIFLOWER
1/4 C. OLIVE OIL
1 CAN (4 OZ.) DICED GREEN CHILIS
2 TSP. BASIL
1 TSP. THYME
1 TSP. SALT
1/4 C. WHOLE WHEAT FLOUR
1 CAN (46 OZ.) TOMATO JUICE

CUT ZUCCHINI IN 1/4 INCH SLICES. CUT
MUSHROOMS IN HALF. CUT FLOWERETTS OF
CAULIFLOWER INTO BITE SIZE PIECES. TOSS
ALL INGREDIENTS TOGETHER BEFORE ADDING
TOMATO JUICE. ADD TOMATO JUICE AND MIX
THOROUGHLY. BRING TO A BOIL THEN SIMME
FOR 30 MINUTES, STIRRING OCCASIONALLY.

FOR EXTRA ZEST, TOP EACH SERVING
WITH 2 TABLESPOONS OF GRATED SHARP
CHEDDAR CHEESE.

SERVES: 6-8

WILDERNESS HOUSE DRESSING

8 OUNCES CREAM CHEESE
1 C. MAYONNAISE
1 TSP. LEMON JUICE
1/2 TSP. SALT
1 C. ZUCCHINI — GROUND
1 TSP. DILL SEED

PUT ALL INGREDIENTS, EXCEPT DILL
SEED, IN BLENDER AND BLEND UNTIL ALMOST
SMOOTH. STIR IN DILL SEED AND CHILL.
TO THIN — ADD MILK.

YIELDS: 3 CUPS

WILDERNESS SALAD

1/2 HEAD LETTUCE - TORN IN SMALL
                    PIECES
1/2 HEAD ROMAINE - TORN IN SMALL
                    PIECES
2 C. ZUCCHINI - GRATED
1 C. FRENCH STYLE GREEN BEANS
3 GREEN ONIONS - MINCED
1/2 C. GRATED MONTEREY JACK CHEESE
3 TBS. BACON BITS
TOSS ALL INGREDIENTS LIGHTLY.
COVER WITH YOUR FAVORITE SALAD
DRESSING. SALT TO TASTE.

SERVES: 4-6

SUMMER SALAD   CRISP AND REFRESHING

1 POUND ZUCCHINI — THINLY SLICED
1 CUCUMBER — PEELED AND THINLY SLICED
1 TSP. SALT
1 TSP. DILL SEED
1 TBS. TARRAGON VINEGAR
1/2 TSP. COARSE BLACK PEPPER
1 C. SOUR CREAM
1 ONION — THINLY SLICED

TOSS ZUCCHINI, CUCUMBER, SALT, DILL SEED, TARRAGON VINEGAR, AND BLACK PEPPER TOGETHER. PLACE IN REFRIGERATOR FOR 20 MINUTES. TOSS WITH SOUR CREAM AND ONIONS. CHILL WELL BEFORE SERVING.

SERVES: 4-6

JULIENNE SALAD

CRUNCHY

1 1/2 POUND ZUCCHINI
1 POUND CARROTS
1 POUND TURNIPS
3/4 C. FRENCH DRESSING

CUT ALL VEGETABLES IN VERY THIN STRIPS, 2 INCHES LONG (JULIENNE). SPRINKLE SALT OVER THE ZUCCHINI AND CHILL FOR 10 MINUTES. BLOT ZUCCHINI DRY — ADD CARROTS AND TURNIPS. TOSS WITH FRENCH DRESSING. CHILL. MOUND ON A VEGETABLE PLATTER TO SERVE.

SERVES: 6-8

ZUCCHINI ASPIC

1 C. HOT WATER
1 3 OZ. PACK LEMON
   GELATIN
1 C. SMALL ZUCCHINI
   THINLY SLICED
1/2 C. FINELY DICED
   CELERY

3/4 CUP SAUTERNE WINE
2 TBS. SUGAR
2 TBS. LEMON JUICE
1/2 TSP. CELERY SEED
1/4 TSP. SALT
2 TBS. GRATED ONION

DISSOLVE GELATIN IN HOT WATER: ADD WINE, LEMON JUICE, SUGAR, AND SALT. STIR WELL. CHILL. WHEN MIXTURE BEGINS TO THICKEN STIR IN REMAINING INGREDIENTS. SPOON INTO 6 INDIVIDUAL OILED MOLDS. CHILL TILL FIRM.

SERVES: 6

HERBED ZUCCHINI TOMATOES

4 FIRM MEDIUM TOMATOES, SLICED
4 MEDIUM ZUCCHINI — THINLY SLICED
1 TSP. SALT
1/4 TSP. COARSE BLACK PEPPER
1/2 TSP. DRIED THYME OR MAJORAM
1/4 C. FINELY SNIPPED PARSLEY
1/4 C. SNIPPED CHIVES
2/3 C. SALAD OIL
1/2 C. TARRAGON VINEGAR

MIX SPICES, VINEGAR, AND OIL. LAYER TOMATOES, ZUCCHINI, AND DRESSING IN A LARGE BOWL. CHILL FOR ONE HOUR. DRAIN AND SERVE ON A PLATTER WITH HALVED HARD COOKED EGGS AND PITTED OLIVES. LINE PLATTER WITH FRILLY LETTUCE. SERVE DRAINED DRESSING ON SIDE.

SERVES: 6

CRUNCHY HAM SANDWICH

SOURDOUGH BREAD
ZUCCHINI-YOUNG, THINLY
   SLICED

SOUR CREAM
HAM-THINLY SLICED
CHIVES

SREAD SOUR CREAM ON SLICE OF BREAD. PLACE LAYER OF SLICED ZUCCHINI THEN SLICED HAM, THEN CHIVES ON BREAD. TOP WITH ANOTHER PIECE OF BREAD AND SOUR CREAM

ZUCCHINI DILL   ABSOLUTELY EXQUISITE

1 1/2 POUNDS MEDIUM ZUCCHINI
2 TSP. SALT
1/4 C. VINEGAR
2 TBS. MARGARINE
2 TBS. WHOLE WHEAT FLOUR
3/4 TSP. DRY DILL WEED
1 C. CREAM

SLICE ZUCCHINI AS YOU WOULD SHOESTRING POTATOES. MARINATE IN VINEGAR AND SALT FOR 30 MINUTES. DRAIN AND BROWN IN MARGARINE FOR 6-8 MINUTES, LEAVING ZUCCHINI SOMEWHAT CRISP. STIR IN FLOUR, DILL WEED, AND CREAM—MAKING A THICK SAUCE. WHEN HOT AND BUBBLING, SERVE.

SERVES: 6

SUCCOTASH

4 C. ZUCCHINI, DICED
2 C. WHOLE KERNEL CORN
1 TBS. MINCED BELL PEPPER
1/4 C. WATER
3 TBS. MARGARINE
1/2 TSP. SALT
1/2 TSP. COARSE GROUND PEPPER

COMBINE ALL INGREDIENTS IN A COVERED PAN. BRING TO A BOIL AND SIMMER FOR 8 MINUTES.

SERVES: 6

ZUCCHINI MOUSSERON

1 POUND SMALL ZUCCHINI
3 C. WATER
2 TSP. SALT
1/2 TSP. DILL SEED
1/2 POUND MUSHROOMS
3 TBS. MARGARINE
1 TBS. FLOUR
1 TBS. ZUCCHINI BROTH
3/4 C. SOUR CREAM

SLICE ZUCCHINI 1/4 INCH THICK. SIMMER IN WATER, SALT, AND DILL SEED FOR ABOUT 8 MINUTES (STILL A BIT CRISP). SLICE MUSHROOMS THIN AND SAUTE IN MARGARINE FOR 5 MINUTES. STIR IN FLOUR - ADD 1 TBS. OF THE BROTH THAT THE ZUCCHINI IS COOKING IN, AND SOUR CREAM. STIR UNTIL GENTLY BUBBLING. DRAIN ZUCCHINI AND STIR INTO SOUR CREAM MIXTURE. SERVE.

SERVES: 6

ZUCCHINI CURRIED RICE

2 C. COOKED BROWN RICE
1/2 TSP. TURMERIC
1 1/2 TSP. CURRY POWDER
2 TBS. HONEY
1 20 OZ. CAN UNSWEETENED
      CRUSHED PINEAPPLE
2 C. GROUND ZUCCHINI
2 TSP. SALT
1/3 C. CHOPPED CHIVES
1/2 C. RAISINS

COOK ZUCCHINI AND CHIVES IN SALTED WATER UNTIL TENDER, ABOUT 3 MINUTES. ADD RAISINS FOR LAST MINUTE OF COOKING. DRAIN WELL. ADD SPICES AND HONEY TO BROWN RICE THEN MIX WITH VEGETABLES. DRAIN PINEAPPLE, MIX IN GENTLY. SERVE HOT.

SERVES: 6

ZUCCHINI-TOMATO KABOBS

PARBOIL 2 MEDIUM SIZE ZUCCHINI FOR 5 MINUTES IN ABOUT 2 CUPS SALTED WATER SEASONED WITH 1/2 TSP. OREGANO. REMOVE AND CUT EACH CROSSWISE IN 4 SECTIONS. THREAD ALTERNATELY WITH CHERRY TOMATOES ON 2 SMALL SKEWERS. BASTE WITH MELTED BUTTER AND COOK ABOUT 8 INCHES ABOVE COALS ON A GRILL FOR ABOUT 10 MINUTES, TURNING AND BASTING FREQUENTLY. JUST BEFORE REMOVING FROM GRILL, SPRINKLE EACH KABOB WITH 1 TBS. OF PARMESAN CHEESE AND A DASH OF SALT AND PEPPER. SERVE IMMEDIATELY.

SERVES: 2

WHITE SAUCE

3 TBS. MARGARINE   3 TBS. WHOLE WHEAT FLOUR
1/4 T.SP. PEPPER   1 T.SP. SALT
2 C. MILK   DASH CAYENNE PEPPER

    MELT MARGARINE, STIR IN FLOUR, SALT, PEPPER AND CAYENNE. BRING TO BUBBLING STAGE, STIRRING CONSTANTLY. SLOWLY ADD MILK, KEEP STIRRING UNTIL IT BUBBLES AND THICKENS.

GOLDEN CASSEROLE

1 T.SP. SALT   1/4 T.SP PEPPER
1/2 T.SP. CELERY SEED   2 C. WHITE SAUCE
3/4 C. BREAD CRUMBS   1/4 C. PARMESAN CHEESE
2 1/2 C. GROUND ZUCCHINI - WELL DRAINED

    COMBINE ZUCCHINI, SPICES, AND WHITE SAUCE. POUR INTO GREASED 1 1/2 QT. CASSEROLE DISH. TOP WITH CHEESE AND BREAD CRUMBS. BAKE AT 350° FOR 30 MINUTES OR UNTIL CASSEROLE BUBBLES AND IS GOLDEN.

SERVES: 4

ZUCCHINI IN SOUR CREAM

4 TO 6 SMALL ZUCCHINI ABOUT 3 CUPS
1 TSP. SALT
1/2 PT. SOUR CREAM
3 TBS. CHOPPED CHIVES
DASH COARSE BLACK PEPPER

SLICE ZUCCHINI AND COOK IN SALTED WATER UNTIL TENDER BUT NOT MUSHY. DRAIN WELL. ADD SOUR CREAM, CHIVES AND PEPPER. MIX CAREFULLY, PUT ON LOW HEAT, STIRRING CONSTANTLY UNTIL HEATED THROUGH.

FOR A DELICIOUS VARIATION, CRUMBLE SIX SLICES OF CRISPLY FRIED BACON INTO ZUCCHINI SOUR CREAM.

SERVES: 4

ZUCCHINI ROMA

4 OR 5 SMALL ZUCCHINI - THINLY
     SLICED   (ABOUT 3 CUPS)
1 TBS. OLIVE OIL
1/2 TSP. SALT
1/4 C. GRATED PARMESAN CHEESE
DASH PEPPER

PUT ZUCCHINI, OIL, AND SEASONINGS IN SKILLET. COVER AND COOK SLOWLY 5 MINUTES. UNCOVER, COOK TURNING SLICES UNTILL BARELY TENDER, ABOUT 5 MINUTES MORE. SPRINKLE WITH CHEESE. TOSS AND SERVE.

SERVES: 4

EVERGREEN ZUCCHINI

4 C. ZUCCHINI, COARSELY GRATED
2 C. PARSLEY FINELY CUT
1/2 TSP. GRATED LEMON PEEL
4 TSP. LEMON JUICE
1/2 TSP. DILL SEED
1/2 TSP. SALT
1/4 TSP. COARSE BLACK PEPPER
1/2 C. (1 CUBE) MARGARINE

MELT MARGARINE IN A LARGE FRYING PAN. ADD ALL OTHER INGREDIENTS AND SAUTE FOR 3 MINUTES – STIRRING CONSTANTLY. (ZUCCHINI SHOULD BE A BIT CRISP) SERVE IMMEDIATELY.

SERVES: 6-8

EGG FOO YUNG

8 EGGS - BEATEN SLIGHTLY 1 C. GROUND ZUCCHINI
1/2 C. CHOPPED GREEN 1/4 C. WHOLE WHEAT FLOUR
     ONIONS 1 TSP. HONEY
2 TSP. SOY SAUCE 1/2 TSP. SALT

MIX ALL INGREDIENTS. FRY IN 4 TBS. OIL USING MIXTURE AS YOU WOULD PANCAKE BATTER. TURN WHEN UNDERSIDE IS BROWN.

YIELDS: 6 PATTIES

HOLIDAY ZUCCHINI
GREAT WITH HAM OR TURKEY

1 1/2 POUNDS SMALL ZUCCHINI
2/3 C. BROWN SUGAR
2 TBS. CORNSTARCH
1/2 TSP. SALT
2 TSP. ORANGE RIND
2 TSP. MARGARINE
1 C. ORANGE JUICE

SLICE ZUCCHINI IN HALF LENGTHWISE. PARBOIL FOR 8 MINUTES IN 2 CUPS WATER AND 1 1/2 TEASPOON SALT. DRAIN WELL. COMBINE BROWN SUGAR, CORNSTARCH, SALT, ORANGE RIND, AND MARGARINE. SLOWLY STIR IN ORANGE JUICE AND BRING TO A BOIL, STIRRING CONSTANTLY. PLACE ZUCCHINI, CUT SIDE UP, IN A GREASED 9 X 9 PAN. POUR SAUCE OVER ZUCCHINI AND BAKE AT 400° FOR 20 MINUTES.

SERVES: 4-6

CORN STUFFED ZUCCHINI

6 MEDIUM ZUCCHINI
1 12 OZ. CAN WHOLE KERNEL CORN
    OR 1 1/2 C. FRESH COOKED CORN
1/4 C. CHOPPED ONION
1 TSP. SALT
1/4 C. CHOPPED CHIVES
1/2 C. GRATED CHEDDAR CHEESE

CUT ZUCCHINI IN HALF LENGTHWISE.
COOK IN SALTED WATER FOR 10 MINUTES.
CAREFULLY REMOVE PULP. DRAIN CORN AND
ZUCCHINI PULP WELL AND COMBINE WITH
SALT ONION   CHIVES. PILE MIXTURE
IN ZUCCHINI SHELLS AND PLACE IN A 13 X
9 INCH PAN. SPRINKLE WITH CHEESE.
BAKE UNCOVERED AT 350° FOR 20 MINUTES.

                            SERVES: 6

FRIED ZUCCHINI (SOOO... GOOD)

2 POUNDS ZUCCHINI
BLEND:
   3 EGGS, BEATEN
   3 TBS. HONEY
   1 TSP. WATER
   1/2 C. WHOLE WHEAT FLOUR
   3/4 TSP. SALT

SLICE ZUCCHINI ABOUT 1/8 INCH THICK.
DIP IN BATTER, THEN FRY IN DEEP OIL
ON MEDIUM HEAT JUST SO IT BUBBLES
GENTLY. TURN SEVERAL TIMES, PIERCING
WITH A FORK OCCASIONALLY UNTIL IT IS
TENDER. DRAIN AND SERVE.
    2 TBS. CELERY SEED MAY BE ADDED TO
BATTER FOR A DISTINCTIVE TASTE.

ZUCCHINI SALERNO

1 POUND ZUCCHINI-SLICED 1/4 INCH THICK
1/2 POUND FRESH MUSHROOMS — THINLY SLICED
1/4 C. MARGARINE.
1 TBS. CORNSTARCH
1/4 C. WATER
1/4 C. SOY SAUCE

MELT MARGARINE IN A SKILLET AND BROWN MUSHROOMS FOR 1 MINUTE. ADD ZUCCHINI AND COOK FOR 2 MORE MINUTES, STIRRING CONSTANTLY. COMBINE THE CORNSTARCH, WATER, AND SOY SAUCE INTO A SMOOTH BROTH. ADD TO THE VEGETABLE MIXTURE AND BRING TO A BOIL WHILE STIRRING. TURN HEAT DOWN AND SIMMER FOR TWO OR THREE MINUTES SO THAT ZUCCHINI IS COOKED, BUT A BIT CRISP.

SERVES: 4

ZUCCHINI CREOLE

1/2 TSP. SALT	2 TBS. MARGARINE
1 BAY LEAF	1/2 C. CHOPPED ONIONS
1/2 TSP. DRIED BASIL LEAVES	1 CLOVE GARLIC FINELY MINCED
1 TSP. SUGAR	1/2 C. CHOPPED GREEN PEPPER
1 LARGE CAN TOMATOES	
2 TBS. FLOUR	2 POUNDS ZUCCHINI

MELT MARGARINE IN SKILLET. ADD ONION, GARLIC, AND GREEN PEPPER. COOK UNTIL TENDER. BLEND IN FLOUR. GRADUALL ADD TOMATOES MIXING WELL. COOK OVER LOW HEAT, STIRRING CONSTANTLY UNTIL THICKENED. REMOVE FROM HEAT. ADD SUGAR, BASIL, BAY LEAF, SALT AND PEPPER. CUT SQUASH IN 1/2 INCH SLICES. (IF USING A LARGE ZUCCHINI THE SKIN MAY BE TOUGH AND SHOULD BE REMOVED.) PLACE ZUCCHINI IN A GREASED 1 1/2 QUART CASSEROLE - POUR IN SAUCE. COVER AND BAKE AT 375° FOR 55 TO 60 MINUTES OR UNTIL TENDER.

SERVES: 4 - 6

STEWED ZUCCHINI

3 LARGE TOMATOES	1/2 C. CHOPPED ONIONS
1 C. DICED CELERY	1/2 GREEN PEPPER - DICED
3 C. ZUCCHINI THINLY SLICED	PINCH OF GARLIC POWDER
	1 TSP. SALT

PLACE ALL INGREDIENTS IN SAUCE PAN, COVER BRING TO BOIL. LET SIMMER FOR ABOUT 15 MINUTES.

LASAGNE   (NO NOODLES)

2 1/2 POUNDS ZUCCHINI
8 OZ. CREAM CHEESE
1 C. COTTAGE CHEESE
1 C. SOUR CREAM
1/4 C. CHOPPED GREEN ONION
1/4 C. CHOPPED GREEN PEPPER
1/2 TSP. OREGANO
1/2 TSP. BASIL
1/2 TSP. ROSEMARY
1/2 TSP. SALT
1 1/2 POUNDS HAMBURGER
1 CAN (8 OZ.) TOMATO SAUCE

SLICE ZUCCHINI - VERY THIN - FROM END
TO END SO THAT YOU HAVE THIN PIECES THE
LENGTH OF THE ZUCCHINI. COMBINE, IN A
BOWL, CREAM CHEESE, COTTAGE CHEESE,
SOUR CREAM, ONION, AND GREEN PEPPER.
BROWN THE HAMBURGER - ADDING SPICES
AND TOMATO SAUCE.

IN A 9 X 12 GREASED CASSEROLE THINLY
LAYER A SMALL AMOUNT OF THE MEAT MIX-
TURE. OVER THE MEAT MAKE A LAYER OF
ZUCCHINI, COVER WITH A SMALL AMOUNT OF
THE CHEESE MIXTURE. REPEAT UNTIL ALL
INGREDIENTS ARE USED, ENDING WITH THE
LAST OF THE MEAT MIXTURE ON TOP.

COVER AND BAKE AT 350° FOR 30 MINUTES.
UNCOVER AND BAKE AT 350° FOR ANOTHER
30 MINUTES.

SERVES: 6-8

CHICKEN-ZUCCHINI SUPPER

2 C. WELL COOKED SLICED ZUCCHINI
2 C. CHOPPED CHICKEN — COOKED
2 C. WHITE SAUCE (PG. 14)
1/2 C. GRATED SWISS CHEESE
1/3 C. WHOLE WHEAT BREAD CRUMBS
1/3 C. PARMESAN CHEESE

DRAIN ZUCCHINI WELL AND PLACE ON BOTTOM OF GREASED CASSEROLE. TOP WITH CHICKEN. ADD SWISS CHEESE TO WHITE SAUCE AND STIR UNTIL MELTED. POUR SAUCE OVER CASSEROLE. SPRINKLE COMBINED BREAD CRUMBS AND PARMESAN ON TOP AND POP INTO OVEN. BAKE AT 350° FOR 30 MINUTES.

SERVES: 4- 6

HAM STUFFED ZUCCHINI

6 MEDIUM ZUCCHINI
2 TBS. CHOPPED ONION
3 TBS. CHOPPED MUSHROOMS (OPTIONAL)
3 TBS. CHOPPED GREEN PEPPER
1 C. CHOPPED COOKED HAM
1/2 TSP. GARLIC SALT
1 C. WHOLE WHEAT BREAD CRUMBS
2 TBS BROTH - IF NEEDED

CUT ZUCCHINI IN HALF LENGTHWISE. SIMMER IN SALTED WATER FOR 10 MINUTES. REMOVE PULP CAREFULLY. COMBINE PULP WITH OTHER INGREDIENT. STUFF ZUCCHINI SHELLS WITH MIXTURE. BAKE AT 350° FOR 30 MINUTES.

SERVES: 4- 6

22

DEEP DISH PIZZA PIE
FOR THE PIZZA LOVER

1 CAN (8 OZ.) CRESCENT ROLLS
1 POUND ZUCCHINI - THINLY SLICED
1 CLOVE GARLIC - MINCED
3 TBS. OIL
1/2 TSP. BASIL
1/2 TSP. OREGANO
1/2 TSP. SALT
2 TSP. FRESH PARSLEY - MINCED
2 EGGS - BEATEN
1 CAN (8 OZ.) TOMATO SAUCE
1 C. GRATED MOZZARELLA CHEESE
1/2 POUND HOT ITALIAN SAUSAGE
————— OR —————
1/4 POUND PEPPERONI - THINLY SLICED

SAUTE ZUCCHINI AND GARLIC IN OIL. ADD SPICES. PLACE TRIANGLES OF CRESCENT ROLL DOUGH IN A DEEP, UNGREASED, PYREX INCH PIE PAN. PRESS PIECES TOGETHER TO FORM A CRUST. SPREAD ON, EVENLY, ZUCCHINI AND SPICE MIXTURE. POUR ON BEATEN EGGS. BAKE FOR 15 MINUTES AT 325°. THEN POUR ON TOMATO SAUCE - SPRINKLE WITH THE CHEESE. IF USING THE ITALIAN SAUSAGE, BROWN FIRST, THEN SPRINKLE OVER THE TOP OF THE PIZZA. WITH PEPPERONI PLACE SLICES EVENLY OVER THE TOP OF THE PIZZA.

BAKE ANOTHER 25 MINUTES AT 325°.

SERVES: 4

ARMENIAN ZUCCHINI

1 POUND GROUND LAMB
2 POUNDS ZUCCHINI
1 CAN 15 OZ. TOMATO
     SAUCE
3/4 TSP. SALT
1/4 TSP. PEPPER

1 C. BROWN RICE,
     UNCOOKED
1 1/2 C. WATER
1/2 C. CHOPPED ONION
3/4 TSP. ALLSPICE

MIX GROUND LAMB, BROWN RICE, ONION, AND SPICES TOGETHER. CUT ZUCCHINI LENGTHWISE — 1/4 INCH THICK. COMBINE WATER AND TOMATO SAUCE. LAYER IN A LARGE HEAVY SKILLET; 1/2 OF ZUCCHINI, 1/2 OF MEAT MIXTURE. POUR 1/2 OF LIQUID OVER LAYERS. REPEAT WITH RE-MAINING INGREDIENTS.

COVER SKILLET — COOK ON MEDIUM HEAT UNTIL CASSEROLE STARTS TO BUBBLE. TURN HEAT DOWN AND SIMMER FOR 45 MINUTES.

SERVES: 6

EASY ZUCCHINI CASSEROLE

1 TSP. SALT	1/4 TSP PEPPER
4 EGGS	2 TBS. MILK
1/4 C. MARGARINE	1 C. GRATED CHEDDAR
2 C. GROUND ZUCCHINI	CHEESE

MIX EGGS, MILK, SEASONINGS, AND MARGARINE IN BLENDER. MIX WITH ZUCCHINI AND CHEESE. POUR INTO GREASED 1 1/2 QUART CASSEROLE DISH. BAKE AT 350° FOR 30 MINUTES OR UNTIL CASSEROLE IS FIRM IN CENTER.

SERVES: 4

SKILLET ZUCCHINI

1 POUND GROUND BEEF
1/4 CHOPPED ONION
1 TBS. WHOLE WHEAT FLOUR
1 C. SEASONED TOMATO SAUCE
3/4 C. WATER
1/4 C. CHOPPED GREEN PEPPER
1 TSP OREGANO
1/2 TSP. CHILI POWDER
1/2 TSP. SALT
3 C. ZUCCHINI THINLY SLICED
1 C. PARMESAN CHEESE

BROWN BEEF AND ONION. SPOON OFF EXCESS FAT. SPRINKLE FLOUR OVER MEAT STIR. ADD TOMATO SAUCE, WATER, GREEN PEPPER, OREGANO, CHILI POWDER, AND SALT. MIX WELL. SEASON ZUCCHINI WITH SALT AND PEPPER. ARRANGE OVER MEAT. COVER; SIMMER TILL ZUCCHINI IS TENDER, ABOUT 15 MINUTES. TOP WITH PARMESAN CHEESE.

SERVES: 6

ZUCCHINI   MILANO

1 POUND GROUND BEEF

3 TBS. OIL

1 ONION - THINLY SLICED

3   8 OZ. CANS TOMATO SAUCE - OR -
      YOUR OWN FRESH PUREED TOMATOES

1 TSP. HONEY

1 C. BURGUNDY, OR OTHER RED WINE

1 TSP. SALT

1/4 TSP. PEPPER

2 POUNDS ZUCCHINI (6 OR 7 MEDIUM)

1/2 TSP. MARJORAM

1/2 TSP. BASIL

1/2 TSP. OREGANO

HEAT OIL. ADD ONION AND BEEF IN SKILLET. COOK UNTIL BROWNED. ADD TOMATO SAUCE, WINE, AND SEASONINGS. COVER; SIMMER GENTLY FOR 30 MINUTES, STIRRING OCCASIONALLY.

WHILE SAUCE IS COOKING: WASH AND TRIM ENDS OFF ZUCCHINI. COOK WHOLE IN BOILING SALTED WATER UNTIL TENDER - ABOUT 15 MINUTES. CUT ZUCCHINI IN HALF LENGTHWISE AND ARRANGE, CUT SIDE UP, IN A SHALLOW CASSEROLE.

POUR SAUCE OVER ZUCCHINI. BAKE AT 350° FOR 45 MINUTES. SERVE WITH PARMESAN CHEESE.

SERVES: 6

ZUCCHINI QUICHE

1/2 POUND JACK CHEESE, GRATED
1 C. GROUND ZUCCHINI
1/4 ONION, CHOPPED
3 EGGS, BEATEN
4 SLICES CRISPLY FRIED BACON
1/2 TSP. SALT
PASTRY FOR A SINGLE PIE CRUST

BREAK UP BACON INTO SMALL PIECES AND COMBINE WITH OTHER INGREDIENTS. POUR INTO A 9 INCH PIE PAN. ROLL PASTRY THIN. CUT 9 INCH DIAMETER ROUND TO LAY OVER QUICHE. CUT A FEW SMALL SLITS IN PASTRY. BAKE AT 350° FOR 45 MINUTES.

DELICIOUS SERVED AS AN EVENING SNACK FOR SPECIAL GUESTS.

SERVES: 4

MEAT LOAF ZUCCHINI

<u>MIX TOGETHER:</u>

- 1 POUND GROUND BEEF
- 1/2 POUND SAUSAGE
- 1/2 C. CHOPPED ONION
- 1/2 C. CHOPPED CELERY
- 1/4 C. CHOPPED BELL PEPPER
- 1 SMALL CAN TOMATO SAUCE -OR-
    - 1/2 C. FRESH PUREED TOMATOES
- 1 EGG
- 1 C. BREAD CRUMBS - OR - 1 C. COOKED
    - BROWN RICE
- 1 1/2 TSP. SALT

CUT ONE LARGE ZUCCHINI (ABOUT 12 INCHES LONG) IN HALF LENGTHWISE. CLEAN OUT SEEDS AND PUNCTURE PULP WITH A FORK SEVERAL TIMES. FILL EACH HALF WITH MEAT MIXTURE, MOUNDING TO OUTER EDGE. PLACE IN 9 X 12 PAN WITH ONE INCH OF WATER IN BOTTOM OF PAN. BAKE AT 350° UNTIL TENDER ABOUT 45 MINUTES. SLICE AND SERVE.

SERVES: 6-8

ZUCCHINI OLÉ

- 1 TSP. SALT
- 1 TSP. CUMIN
- 1/2 ONION, SLICED
- 1/2 POUND GRATED JACK CHEESE
- 3 C. ZUCCHINI - THINLY SLICED
- 1 7 OZ. CAN CHILI SALSA

PLACE ALL INGREDIENTS, EXCEPT CHEESE, IN A SAUCE PAN. SIMMER FOR 10 OR 15 MINUTES UNTIL ZUCCHINI IS TENDER AND LIQUID HAS EVAPORATED. GENTLY STIR IN GRATED CHEESE. SERVE IMMEDIATELY.

SERVES: 4

ZUCCHINI OMELET

    4 EGGS
    1/2 TSP. SALT
    2 TBS. CHOPPED ONION
    1/2 C. GRATED CHEESE
    1/2 C. COOKED ZUCCHINI DRAINED

BEAT EGGS AND SALT WITH A FORK. POUR INTO A HOT, GREASED, 9 INCH SKILLET. THEN, COVER AND TURN HEAT TO LOW FOR 2 MINUTES. THEN PUT ZUCCHINI, ONION, AND GRATED CHEESE ON ONE HALF OF THE EGGS. WITH SPATULA GENTLY FOLD OTHER HALF OF EGGS OVER THE PORTION COVERED WITH THE MIXTURE. PUT LID ON SKILLET FOR ANOTHER 3 OR 4 MINUTES, UNTIL OMELET IS FIRM AND CHEESE HAS MELTED. SERVE WITH SOUR CREAM OR CHILI SALSA.

SERVES: 5

ZUCCHINI SCRAMBLED EGGS

USE ABOVE INGREDIENTS. PLACE ALL INGREDIENTS EXCEPT GRATED CHEESE INTO HOT GREASED SKILLET. SCRAMBLE TOGETHER GENTLY UNTIL EGGS ARE DONE. FOLD IN CHEESE. SERVE WITH SOUR CREAM OR CHILI SALSA.

SPAGHETTI

1 POUND HOT ITALIAN SAUSAGE
2 POUND ZUCCHINI - THINLY SLICED
1 CAN (16 OZ.) TOMATO SAUCE
3/4 TSP. BASIL
1/2 TSP. ROSEMARY
3/4 TSP. SALT
1/4 C. PARMESAN GRATED CHEESE

BROWN SAUSAGE IN A HEAVY SKILLET.
ADD ZUCHINNI, TOMATO SAUCE, AND SPICES
COVER AND SIMMER FOR 30 MINUTES.
JUST BEFORE SERVING MIX IN CHEESE.
POUR OVER 8 OUNCES OF COOKED SPAGHETT

SERVES: 6

WILDERNESS ZUCCHINI CASSEROLE

2 C. SLICED ZUCCHINI   1/4 C. CHOPPED
3/4 TSP SALT   PARSLEY
1/2 ONION-GRATED   1 EGG, BEATEN
1 C. MILK   1 CLOVE GARLIC, MINCED

SLICE ZUCCHINI THIN, PARBOIL IN
SALTED WATER, DRAIN, AND PLACE IN A
SHALLOW BAKING DISH. BLEND GARLIC,
EGG, MILK, SALT, AND PARSLEY. POUR
OVER ZUCCHINI AND SPRINKLE ONIONS
OVER TOP. SET BAKING DISH IN A PAN
OF HOT WATER. BAKE AT 350° UNTIL
CUSTARD SETS, ABOUT 30 MINUTES.
SERVES: 4

STROGONOFF

1 POUND CHICKEN LIVERS CUT IN HALVES
1/2 POUND MUSHROOMS — THINLY SLICED
1 1/2 POUND ZUCCHINI - THINLY SLICED
1/2 C. CHOPPED ONIONS
3 TBS. MARGARINE
1/2 C. DRY SHERRY
1 TBS. WORCHESTERSHIRE SAUCE
3/4 TSP. SALT
2 C. SOUR CREAM

BROWN CHICKEN LIVERS, MUSHROOMS, AND ONIONS, IN MARGARINE. ADD SHERRY, WORCHESTERSHIRE, SALT, AND ZUCCHINI. SIMMER FOR 30 MINUTES UNTIL ZUCCHINI IS VERY TENDER. JUST BEFORE SERVING STIR IN SOUR CREAM. SERVE OVER BROWN RICE.

SERVES: 6

LENDE SUPREME

1 1/2 POUNDS ZUCCHINI — THINLY SLICED
2 CANS 4 OZ. GREEN CHILIS
1/2 POUND CHEDDAR CHEESE — GRATED
1/2 POUND JACK CHEESE — GRATED

IN A 2 QUART GREASED CASSEROLE,
LAYER ZUCCHINI, CHILIS, AND CHEESE
THREE TIMES.

COMBINE THE FOLLOWING AND POUR
OVER THE CASSEROLE:
2/3 C. WHOLE WHEAT FLOUR
3 EGGS — BEATEN
1/2 C. MILK
1/2 TSP. BAKING POWDER
3/4 TSP. SALT
COVER TIGHTLY AND BAKE AT 375°
FOR 45 MINUTES.

SERVES: 6-8

CHINESE EGG ROLLS

1 POUND GROUND BEEF
1 LARGE ONION — CHOPPED
2 CLOVES GARLIC — MASHED
4 C. ZUCCHINI — CHOPPED
2 C. CABBAGE — CHOPPED
3 TBS. CORNSTARCH
3 TBS. SOY SAUCE
1 TBS. HONEY
1 TSP. SALT
1 PACKAGE (16 OZ.) EGG ROLL SKINS
1 EGG — BEATEN

FRY GROUND BEEF UNTIL BROWN. ADD ONION AND GARLIC — COOK FOR 1 MINUTE. ADD ZUCCHINI AND CABBAGE — COOK AN ADDITIONAL 2 MINUTES. MIX CORNSTARCH, SOY SAUCE, HONEY, AND SALT. TOSS WITH MEAT MIXTURE AND COOK 1 MORE MINUTE. COOL. FILL EACH EGG ROLL SKIN WITH 2 HEAPING TABLESPOONS OF THE VEGETABLE — MEAT MIXTURE. ROLL AND SEAL EDGES WITH BEATEN EGG. DEEP FAT FRY FOR 4 MINUTES UNTIL CRISP AND GOLDEN. (EGG ROLLS CAN BE FROZEN AND REHEATED BY BAKING.)
SERVE WITH SOY SAUCE, SWEET'N SOUR OR OUR FAVORITE — HOT SWEET MUSTARD SAUCE.
HOT SWEET MUSTARD SAUCE
1/2 C. MUSTARD
4 TSP HORSERADISH
2 TBS. HONEY

YIELDS: 24 ROLLS

33

ZUCCHINI AND EGGPLANT

4 SLICES BACON
1/2 C. SLIVERED ALMONDS (OPTIONAL)
1 TBS. OIL
1 POUND ZUCCHINI - DICED
1 POUND EGGPLANT - DICED
1 LARGE ONION - DICED
2 TBS. FLOUR
1 CAN (16 OZ) DICED TOMATOES
1 TSP. MINCED GARLIC
1 1/2 TSP. SALT
1/4 TSP. COARSE PEPPER
1 TSP. BASIL
1/2 POUND SLICED SWISS CHEESE

CUT BACON IN 1 INCH PIECES. SAUTE
WITH ALMONDS IN A SKILLET UNTIL THE BACON
HAS SLIGHTLY BROWNED - NOT CRISP. REMOVE
BOTH FROM SKILLET AND SET ASIDE. ADD
OIL, ZUCCHINI, EGGPLANT, AND ONION TO
THE SKILLET AND SAUTE FOR 5 MINUTES.
STIR IN FLOUR - ADD TOMATOES, THEN SPICE
HEAT TO BUBBLING - THEN POUR INTO A 3
QUART CASSEROLE. TOP THE INGREDIENTS
WITH SWISS CHEESE, THEN SPRINKLE
BACON ALMOND MIXTURE OVER THE TOP.
BAKE AT 375° FOR 30 MINUTES OR UNTIL
VEGETABLES ARE TENDER.

SERVES: 6

ZUCCHINI ITALIANO

2 EGGS, WELL BEATEN
1/2 C. WHOLE WHEAT FLOUR
2 C. SPAGHETTI SAUCE OR PIZZA SAUCE
2 C. GRATED MONTEREY JACK CHEESE
1 LARGE ZUCCHINI — ABOUT 12 INCHES

SLICE ZUCCHINI ABOUT 1/8 INCH
THICK. DIP IN FLOUR. THEN EGGS FRY
UNTIL GOLDEN BROWN AND TENDER.
LAYER ZUCCHINI IN 9 X 12 PAN. POUR
SPAGHETTI OR PIZZA SAUCE OVER TOP.
SPREAD CHEESE EVENLY ON TOP.
BAKE AT 350° UNTIL CASSEROLE
BUBBLES — ABOUT 30 MINUTES. (PARMESAN
CHEESE MAY BE SUBSTITUTED FOR
MONTEREY JACK — BUT USE ONLY
1/2 CUP.)   A FILLING MAIN DISH!

SERVES: 6

TAMALE PIE

1/2 POUND HAMBURGER
1 POUND ZUCCHINI
1/4 C. DICED ONION
1 1/2 TSP. CHILI POWDER
1/2 TSP. CUMIN
1 1/2 TSP SALT
1 1/2 C. WHOLE KERNEL CORN
1 CAN (28 OZ) DICED TOMATOES
3/4 C. CORN MEAL
1 C. GRATED CHEDDAR CHEESE (OPTIONAL)

SLICE ZUCCHINI 1/8 INCH THICK.
BROWN HAMBURGER, ZUCCHINI, AND ONION IN
OIL.   ADD SPICES, CORN,   TOMATOES,
AND CORN MEAL - MIX WELL. POUR INTO A
9 X 9 BAKING DISH. TOP WITH GRATED
CHEESE (OPTIONAL). BAKE AT 350° FOR
30 MINUTES.

SERVES: 6 - 8

MACARONI PARISIAN

    2 QUARTS WATER
    2 TSP. SALT
    8 OZ. MACARONI
    1/2 C. CHOPPED PARSLEY
    2 C. GRATED ZUCCHINI
    2 CLOVES MINCED GARLIC

    BRING SALTED WATER TO A BOIL.
ADD MACARONI AND COOK UNTIL TENDER.
DRAIN. RETURN TO PAN OVER MEDIUM
HEAT. STIR IN PARSLEY, ZUCCHINI AND
GARLIC. TURN HEAT OFF. PLACE LID ON
PAN WHILE PREPARING SAUCE.

SAUCE

        HEAT TOGETHER IN A SKILLET.
        STIR UNTIL SMOOTH.

        2 OZ. GRATED JACK CHEESE
        1/2 C. PARMESAN CHEESE
        1/3 C. OLIVE OIL
        1/3 C. MILK

    POUR SAUCE OVER MACARONI.
TOSS LIGHTLY AND SERVE.

                    SERVES: 6

GARDEN SOUFFLÉ

3 C. GRATED ZUCCHINI
1 1/2 C. CORN
1/2 C. MINCED BELL PEPPER
1/4 C. CHOPPED GREEN ONION
1 TBS. BUTTER
1 TSP. SALT

STIR FRY IN SKILLET FOR 3 MINUTES.

6 TBS. BUTTER
6 TBS. FLOUR
1 TSP. SALT
1/2 TSP. COARSE BLACK PEPPER
1 1/4 C. MILK
6 EGGS — SEPARATED
1/2 C. GRATED JACK CHEESE

MELT BUTTER IN SAUCEPAN. BLEND IN FLOUR AND SPICES. COOK UNTIL BUBBLY. SLOWLY STIR IN MILK. STIR WHILE MIXTURE THICKENS. COOK FOR 3 MINUTES. BEAT EGG YOLKS. POUR HOT MIXTURE INTO EGG YOLKS. FOLD IN CHEESE AND VEGETABLES. BEAT EGG WHITES UNTIL STIFF. FOLD INTO VEGETABLE MIXTURE.

POUR INTO 2 QUART BUTTERED SOUFFLE DISH OR BUTTERED CASSEROLE.

BAKE AT 350 FOR 55 MINUTES — UNTIL GOLDEN AND PUFFY.

SERVES: 6

ZUCCHINI FRITTERS

1/2 C. FLOUR
1 TSP. BAKING POWDER
1/4 TSP. SALT
3 EGGS-WELL BEATEN
1/4 C. GRATED PARMESAN CHEESE
1/4 C. MINCED ONIONS
1 C. GRATED ZUCCHINI

COMBINE INGREDIENTS IN ORDER GIVEN. USE 2 TABLESPOONS OF BATTER FOR EACH FRITTER. DROP BATTER ON A HOT SKILLET. COOK UNTIL BROWNED. TURN FRITTER OVER AND BROWN OTHER SIDE.

MAKES: 16 FRITTERS

ENCHILADAS

        1/4 C. OIL
        1 1/2 POUNDS ZUCCHINI
        2 CLOVES GARLIC - MINCED
        1 ONION - DICED
        1 BELL PEPPER - MINCED
        1 4 OZ. CAN DICED GREEN CHILIS
        1 4 OZ. CAN SLICED OLIVES
        2 1/2 C. GRATED CHEDDAR CHEESE
        2 10 OZ. CANS ENCHILADA SAUCE
        1 DOZEN CORN TORTILLAS

    CUT ZUCCHINI IN 1/2 INCH SLICES.
HEAT OIL IN SKILLET AND STIR FRY ZUCCHIN.
GARLIC, ONION AND BELL PEPPER FOR 5
MINUTES. ADD CHILIS, OLIVES AND 1 1/2
CUPS CHEDDAR CHEESE.

    HEAT ENCHILADA SAUCE UNTIL STEAMIN.
DIP EACH TORTILLA IN SAUCE UNTIL SOFT.
SPOON THE VEGETABLE MIXTURE INTO THE
CENTER OF EACH TORTILLA AND ROLL CLOSE
ARRANGE IN A 9 X 13 PAN. COVER ALL OF
THE ENCHILADAS WITH THE REMAINING SAUCE
AND CHEESE.

    BAKE AT 350° FOR 20 MINUTES.

                        SERVES: 4

ALMA'S SPECIALTY

4 EGGS, BEATEN   1/2 C. MILK
1 TSP. SALT   3 TBS. FLOUR
1 POUND GRATED JACK   1 TBS. BAKING POWDER
    CHEESE   1/2 C. BREAD CRUMBS
1 1/2 POUNDS ZUCCHINI — CUT IN 1/2 INCH SLICES

COOK ZUCCHINI IN A VERY SMALL AMOUNT OF WATER FOR 5 MINUTES. DRAIN AND COOL.

PUT EGGS, MILK, SALT, BAKING POWDER, AND FLOUR IN LARGE BOWL AND MIX WELL. STIR ZUCCHINI AND CHEESE INTO LIQUID. PLACE IN GREASED 2 QUART CASSEROLE. SPRINKLE WITH BREAD CRUMBS. DOT WITH MARGARINE. BAKE AT 350° FOR 35 MINUTES. CHECK FOR DONENESS WITH A KNIFE AS YOU DO FOR A CUSTARD.

SERVES: 4

41

NUTRITIOUS-DELICIOUS COOKIES

STIR TOGETHER DRY INGREDIENTS:

1 1/2 C. FLOUR   1 TSP. BAKING SODA
1/2 TSP SALT   1/2 TSP CINNAMON
1/2 TSP. NUTMEG   1/4 TSP. CLOVES

PUT FOLLOWING IN BOWL — BEAT FOR 3 MINUTES

1/2 C. MARGARINE   2/3 C. HONEY
1 C. GROUND ZUCCHINI   1 EGG, BEATEN

COMBINE BLENDED MIXTURE WITH DRY INGREDIENTS. ADD THE FOLLOWING:
1/2 C. ROLLED OATS
1 C. DATES, FINELY CHOPPED
1 C. WALNUTS, CHOPPED
1/2 C. SHREDDED COCONUT (OPTIONAL)
DROP BY HEAPING SPOONFULS ONTO AN OILED COOKIE SHEET. BAKE AT 325° FOR 15 MINUTES UNTIL COOKIES ARE GOLDEN.

ZUCCHINI SPICE PIE
(MUCH LIKE PUMPKIN)

PUT IN BLENDER:

3/4 C. BROWN SUGAR   1 TBS. FLOUR
1 1/2 C. GROUND ZUCCHINI   1/2 TSP. SALT
    WELL DRAINED   1 TSP. GINGER
1 1/2 C. EVAPORATED MILK   1 1/2 TSP. CINNAMON
2 TBS. MOLASSES   2 EGGS
1/4 TSP. NUTMEG   1/2 TSP. CLOVES

BLEND AT HIGH SPEED FOR AT LEAST 1 MINUTE. POUR INTO UNBAKED PASTRY LINED 9 INCH PIE PAN. BAKE AT 450° FOR 10 MINUTES — THEN TURN OVEN TO 350° FOR 45 MINUTES.

DATE NUT TORTE

2 C. ZUCCHINI — GRATED
1 C. DATES — DICED
1/2 C. CHOPPED WALNUTS
1 C. BROWN SUGAR
2 EGGS, BEATEN
1 TBS. OIL
1 TSP. VANILLA
1/2 TSP. SALT
1 TSP. CINNAMON
3/4 C. WHOLE WHEAT FLOUR
2 1/2 TSP. BAKING POWDER

BEAT EGGS, BROWN SUGAR, OIL, VANILLA, SALT, AND CINNAMON IN A BOWL. SLOWLY STIR IN FLOUR AND BAKING POWDER, WHICH HAS BEEN COMBINED. STIR IN ZUCCHINI, DATES, AND WALNUTS — POUR INTO A GREASED 9 X 9 PAN. BAKE AT 350° FOR 60 MINUTES. LET SIT FOR AN HOUR BEFORE SERVING. CUT INTO SQUARES. MAY BE SERVED WITH WHIPPED CREAM.

SERVES: 9

UNIQUE CHOCOLATE CAKE

STIR TOGETHER DRY INGREDIENTS:

2 1/2 C. WHOLE WHEAT FLOUR
2 1/2 TSP. BAKING POWDER

1/2 C. COCOA
1 TSP. SALT
1 1/2 TSP. BAKING SODA
1 TSP. CINNAMON

PUT FOLLOWING IN BOWL — BEAT FOR 3 MINUTES

3/4 C. SOFT MARGARINE
2 TSP. VANILLA
2 C. GROUND ZUCCHINI

2 C. HONEY
3 EGGS
1/3 C. MILK

COMBINE BOWL MIXTURE WITH DRY INGREDIENTS. BAKE IN 9 X 12 INCH GREASED PAN AT 350° FOR 35 TO 40 MINUTES. TEST WITH TOOTHPICK. AFTER CAKE IS COOL FROST WITH YOUR FAVORITE FROSTING — OR — POUR WILDERNESS GLAZE OVER CAKE.

WILDERNESS GLAZE

3/4 C. HONEY
2 TBS. COARSELY SHREDDED ORANGE PEEL
1/3 C. WARM WATER

MIX TOGETHER AND DRIBBLE EVENLY OVER TOP OF CAKE. LET STAND 1/2 HOUR PRIOR TO SERVING.

SPICE CAKE

STIR TOGETHER DRY INGREDIENTS:

2 1/2 C. WHOLE WHEAT FLOUR
1 TSP. SALT
1 1/2 TSP. CINNAMON

2 1/2 TSP. BAKING POWDER
1 1/2 TSP. BAKING SODA
1/2 TSP. CLOVE
1 TSP. NUTMEG

PUT FOLLOWING IN BOWL— BEAT FOR 3 MINUTES.

2 C. HONEY
2 TSP. VANILLA
2 C. GROUND ZUCCHINI

3 EGGS, BEATEN
1/4 C. MILK
3/4 C. MARGARINE

ADD WET MIXTURE TO DRY INGREDIENTS. STIR UNTIL COMPLETELY MIXED.
BAKE AT 350° IN TWO 9 INCH CAKE PANS FOR 35 MINUTES—OR—ONE 9 X 12 INCH CAKE PAN FOR 45 MINUTES. TEST WITH TOOTHPICK FOR DONENESS.

HONEY CUSTARD

PUT IN BLENDER:

1 1/2 C. GROUND ZUCCHINI WELL DRAINED
1 1/2 TSP. CINNAMON
1/2 TSP. CLOVES
1/2 TSP. SALT
2 EGGS

1 C. HONEY
2 TBS. MOLASSES
1/4 TSP. NUTMEG
1 TSP. GINGER
1 TBS. FLOUR
1 C. EVAPORATED MILK

BLEND AT HIGH SPEED FOR AT LEAST 1 MINUTE. POUR MIXTURE INTO 9" PIE PAN— PYREX IS BEST. BAKE AT 450° FOR 5 MINUTES—THEN TURN OVEN TO 350° FOR 30 MINUTES.
THIS IS ALSO DELICIOUS— POUR MIXTURE INTO AN UNBAKED PIE SHELL AND BAKE FOLLOWING SAME DIRECTIONS.

ZUCCHINI PANCAKES
(HEALTHY — DELICIOUS)

1 1/2 C. WHOLE WHEAT FLOUR
2 EGGS — BEATEN
3/4 TSP. SALT
1 C. MILK
3 TSP. BAKING POWDER
1 TBS. HONEY
3 TBS. OIL
1 C. GROUND ZUCCHINI

COMBINE EGGS WITH OTHER LIQUIDS. ADD ZUCCHINI THEN SIFTED DRY INGREDIENTS, STIRRING VERY LITTLE. SPOON BATTER ONTO LIGHTLY GREASED GRIDDLE AT MEDIUM HEAT. TURN CAKES WHEN THEY HAVE STARTED TO BUBBLE. CONTINUE COOKING TO BROWN OTHER SIDE. TOP WITH WILDERNESS SYRUP.

WILDERNESS SYRUP:

MELT TOGETHER EQUAL AMOUNTS OF BUTTER AND HONEY. SERVE WARM.

COUNTRY BREAD (OR MUFFINS)

1 1/2 C. GROUND ZUCCHINI — DRAINED
4 TBS. DRIED MINCED ONION
1/2 C. GRATED SHARP CHEDDAR
        CHEESE
2 EGGS - BEATEN
1/3 C. OIL
2 TBS. HONEY
1 C. BUTTERMILK
3 C. WHOLE WHEAT FLOUR
4 TSP. BAKING POWDER
1/2 TSP. BAKING SODA
1 1/2 TSP. SALT

MIX TOGETHER WHOLE WHEAT FLOUR, BAKING POWDER, BAKING SODA, AND SALT. COMBINE FIRST SEVEN INGREDIENTS TOGETHER — THEN ADD TO THE FLOUR MIXTURE. SPREAD IN A GREASED 9 X 5 X 3 LOAF PAN. BAKE AT 350° FOR 35 MINUTES. LOAF WILL PULL AWAY SLIGHTLY FROM SIDES OF THE PAN. LET SIT FOR 10 MINUTES BEFORE REMOVING FROM PAN.

YIELD: 1 LOAF

FOR MUFFINS: SPREAD INTO GREASED MUFFIN TINS FILLING 2/3 FULL. BAKE AT 350° FOR 20 MINUTES. MUFFINS SHOULD BE BROWN AND CRISP LOOKING.

YIELD: 18 MUFFINS

ZUCCHINI BREAD OUR FAVORITE

MIX IN BOWL:

   3 EGGS - BEATEN
   1 C. OIL
   2 C. BROWN SUGAR
   2 C. GROUND ZUCCHINI
   2 TSP. VANILLA
   1 TSP. SALT

COMBINE IN A SEPARATE BOWL:

   3 C. WHOLE WHEAT FLOUR
   1 TSP. BAKING SODA
   1/4 TSP. BAKING POWDER
   1 TBS. CINNAMON
   1/2 C. CHOPPED NUTS

ADD WET INGREDIENTS TO DRY INGREDIENTS - MIX WELL. POUR INTO 2 5 X 8 OILED LOAF PANS. BAKE AT 375° FOR 70 MINUTES.

FOR BEAUTY, SPRINKLE WITH ADDITIONAL FINELY CHOPPED NUTS JUST BEFORE BAKING.

YIELDS: 2 LOAVES

TO MAKE ZUCCHINI BREAD WITH HONEY INSTEAD OF SUGAR .... REPLACE BROWN SUGAR WITH 1 1/2 CUPS OF HONEY AND DECREASE THE OIL TO 3/4 CUP.

CORN BREAD

3/4 C. WHOLE WHEAT FLOUR
3/4 C. CORN MEAL
1 1/2 TSP. BAKING POWDER
1/2 TSP. SALT
1 TBS. HONEY
1 EGG-BEATEN
2 TBS. OIL
3/4 C. MILK
3/4 C. ZUCCHINI - GROUND

COMBINE DRY INGREDIENTS. BEAT EGG, OIL, AND MILK TOGETHER. ADD ZUCCHINI AND LIQUID MIXTURE TO DRY INGREDIENTS - STIR WELL. POUR BATTER INTO AN OILED 9 X 9 PAN. BAKE 25 MINUTES IN A 400° OVEN.

SERVES: 9

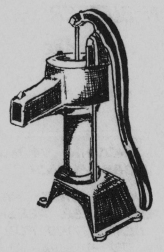

DILL PICKLED ZUCCHINI

HEAT TO BOILING:

3 QUARTS WATER
3/4 C. PICKLING SALT
1 QUART CIDER VINEGAR

IN QUART JARS FIT AS MANY SMALL ZUCCHINIS AS POSSIBLE. TO EACH JAR ADD:

3/4 TSP DILL WEED   1/4 TSP. CRUSHED
1 CLOVE GARLIC   RED PEPPER
1/2 TSP ALUM   3/4 TSP. DILL SEED

POUR HOT LIQUID INTO JARS. SEAL WITH KERR LIDS. PUT IN CANNING POT WITH TOPS IMMERSED IN WATER, SIMMERING FOR 15 MINUTES. TAKE OUT AND LET SIT FOR TWO WEEKS PRIOR TO USING.

THESE WILL NOT BE QUITE AS FIRM AS CUCUMBER PICKLES, BUT EVERY BIT AS DELICIOUS.

ZUCCHINI BREAD-N-BUTTER PICKLES

1 QUART APPLE CIDER VINEGAR
3 1/2 C. SUGAR
3 TBS. PICKLING SALT
2 TSP. CELERY SEED
1 TSP. TURMERIC
2 TSP. MUSTARD SEED
4 QUARTS SLICED ZUCCHINI 1/4 INCH THICK
1 QUART SLICED ONIONS 1/4 INCH THICK

BRING VINEGAR, SUGAR, SALT AND SPICES TO A BOIL. POUR OVER FRESHLY SLICED VEGETABLES AND LET STAND FOR 1 HOUR. BRING MIXTURE TO A BOIL AND BOIL 10 MINUTES.

PACK HOT INTO HOT STERILIZED JARS. SEAL AT ONCE. DO NOT OPEN FOR TWO WEEKS.

ZUCCHINI HOT SALSA

10 C. GROUND ZUCCHINI
3 C. GROUND ONIONS
3 1 2 C. GROUND ANAHEIM PEPPERS
(ABOUT 25)

ADD 5 TBS. OF SALT TO MIXTURE AND
LET SIT OVERNIGHT. NEXT MORNING RINSE
THOROUGHLY USING COLLANDER OR LARGE
STRAINER. MIX TOGETHER WELL WITH:

1 TSP. GARLIC POWDER	1 TBS. CRUSHED RED
1 TBS. CUMIN	PEPPER
1 C. BROWN SUGAR	1 TSP. NUTMEG
1 TBS. CORNSTARCH	1 TSP. COARSE PEPPER
2 TSP. DRY MUSTARD	1 TSP. TURMERIC
2 C. VINEGAR	5 C. GROUND TOMATOES

MIX WELL. BOIL FOR 30 MINUTES. SEAL
IN HOT JARS.

SPICY HAMBURGER RELISH

10 C. GROUND ZUCCHINI
3 C. GROUND ONIONS
4 GREEN PEPPERS — GROUND

ADD 5 TBS. OF SALT TO MIXTURE AND
LET SIT OVERNIGHT. NEXT MORNING RINSE
THOROUGHLY AND MIX WELL WITH:

3 C. BROWN SUGAR	1 TSP. NUTMEG
1 TBS. CORNSTARCH	1 TSP. COURSE PEPPER
1 TSP. TURMERIC	10 SMALL RED PEPPERS
1 C. VINEGAR	GROUND
1 TSP. DRY MUSTARD	

MIX WELL. BOIL FOR 30 MINUTES.
SEAL IN HOT JARS.

MARMALADE

- 3 POUNDS ZUCCHINI
- 4 ORANGES
- 1 LEMON
- 1/4 TSP. SODA
- 10 C. SUGAR
- 1 BOTTLE (6 OZ) FRUIT PECTIN

COARSELY GRIND ZUCCHINI, ORANGES, AND LEMON. COMBINE IN A PAN WITH SODA AND SUGAR. LET SIT FOR 30 MINUTES. BRING TO A ROLLING BOIL—WHILE STIRRING, THEN SIMMER FOR 60 MINUTES, OCCASIONALLY SKIMMING OFF THE FOAM THAT FORMS ON TOP. REMOVE FROM HEAT AND ADD PECTIN—STIRRING WELL. LADLE INTO HOT JARS AND COVER AT ONCE WITH 1/8 INCH HOT PARAFFIN OR SEAL WITH CANNING LIDS.

YIELDS: 6 PINTS

OR......... IF YOU WOULD RATHER MAKE YOUR MARMALADE WITH HONEY ————

SUBSTITUE:
- 8 C. HONEY FOR SUGAR
- 6 OZ. DRY PECTIN FOR BOTTLED PECTIN

FOLLOW DIRECTIONS ABOVE, BUT AFTER ADDING THE DRY PECTIN, BOIL HARD FOR 4 MINUTES; THEN LADLE INTO JARS.

HOW TO DRY ZUCCHINI

FOR THOSE OF YOU THAT DON'T HAVE A FREEZER TO STORE YOUR ZUCCHINI IN, OR THOSE OF YOU THAT ARE "SURVIVAL FOOD" CONSCIOUS, YOU MIGHT LIKE TO TRY DRIED ZUCCHINI.

WE AT WILDERNESS HOUSE HAVEN'T EXPERIMENTED A GREAT DEAL WITH USING DRIED ZUCCHINI BUT HAVE FOUND THAT IT IS GREAT TOSSED INTO HOT SOUPS OR STEWS. AND, BELIEVE IT OR NOT, WE FIND OUR CHILDREN MUNCHING ON IT AS A SNACK.

USE YOUR VERY BEST, FRESH ZUCCHINI. WASH, TRIM ENDS AND STEMS, AND SLICE 1/8 INCH THICK. PUT SINGLE LAYER, NOT LETTING PIECES TOUCH EACH OTHER, ON A COOKIE SHEET COVERED WITH WAX PAPER.

PUT COOKIE SHEETS IN OVEN AT 140 — 150° FOR 4 TO 6 HOURS. IF TEMPERATURE IS TOO LOW, ZUCCHINI WILL SOUR; IF IT IS TOO HIGH, THE WALLS WILL BURST AND THE JUICE WILL LEAK OUT. TURN PIECES AT LEAST ONCE DURING DRYING.

DRYING IS FINISHED WHEN THE PIECES ARE AS BRITTLE AS POTOTO CHIPS. THEY SHOULD NOT BE PLIABLE. ALL MOISTURE MUST BE GONE OR ZUCCHINI WILL ATTRACT BACTERIA AND SPOIL.

YOU WILL NOTICE THAT YOUR DRIED ZUCCHINI WILL HAVE A MORE INTENSE FLAVOR. YOU WILL HAVE ABOUT 1 OZ. DRIED PER ONE POUND FRESH ZUCCHINI.

STORE IN AIR TIGHT PLASTIC BAGS, SEALED; OR AIR TIGHT JARS.

ENJOY

HOW TO FREEZE ZUCCHINI

WASH, TRIM ENDS, AND SLICE ACCORDING TO YOUR PREFERENCE. YOU NEED NOT PARBOIL ZUCCHINI. SIMPLY PLACE THE SLICED ZUCCHINI IN DOUBLE PLASTIC BAGS AND SEAL. WHEN DEFROSTED THE ZUCCHINI WILL NOT BE AS FIRM AND CRISP AS FRESH ZUCCHINI, WHICH IS ALSO TRUE OF COMMERCIALLY FROZEN ZUCCHINI.

REFER TO WILDERNESS HOUSE TIPS FOR FREEZING OF GRATED OR GROUND ZUCCHINI.

NOTES

IF YOU HAVE TRIED ALL OF
OUR WILDERNESS HOUSE
RECIPES YOU WILL HAVE USED

93 POUNDS

OF ZUCCHINI

56